IDENTITY IN CHRIST
GROUP BIBLE STUDY

WRITTEN BY Jaymie Dieterle

RELEVANCE
SERIES

Identity in Christ: Group Bible Study
Written by Jaymie Dieterle
© 2020 Warner Press Inc.

Requests for information should be sent to:
Warner Press Inc.
P.O. Box 2499
Anderson, IN 46018
www.warnerpress.org

Kevin Stiffler • Editor
S. Katie Miller • Layout & Design

CONTENTS

The Warner Press *Relevance* Group Bible Studies provide intriguing examinations of topics using the whole of the Scriptures. The guides incorporate various stories and activities to introduce and apply the subject matter, with a Bible study component at the heart of each session. Our goal is to show life-long believers and those new to the faith how to know the Lord intimately while encouraging them to step out and join him in his work with miraculous results.

These flexible studies are ideal for any setting. We know that time is a valuable commodity in today's society, and that's why each book consists of five or six short lessons intended to meet the group's scheduling needs.

I Am God's Child

Romans 8:13–17; Galatians 3:26 — 4:7; 1 John 3:1

Main Point

Because of God's lavish love and Christ's death on the cross for our sins and resurrection to life, we are sons and daughters of God and co-heirs with Jesus.

Background

Even folks who have walked with God for years can struggle with the idea that God loves them no matter what. Maybe it's shame over the sins of their past. Maybe they've never felt they were loveable. Maybe they had a traumatic childhood that makes it difficult for them to see God as a loving Father. Whatever gets in the way of us trusting and living from a place of love and security with God, the Bible is clear. God loves us. He is the perfect parent. We have been adopted into his family and nothing can separate us from him.

God's Children

"I can't stop thinking about the song we sang this morning about being a child of God. I always thought of God as watching from above so he could punish us like a parent. But this song made being a child of God sound like a good thing. I don't get that."

Caitlin was new to the church. The pastor seemed open and honest, so she felt safe bringing her questions to him.

The pastor smiled. "That's a great question! But the answer might take a while. My wife, Tonya, and I are headed out for lunch. Why don't you join us—and bring your questions!"

Caitlin hesitated. Pastor Mike might not realize how long it had been since she had been to church and how little she knew about the Bible. But the words "Yes, I'd love that" were out before she could second-guess them.

Has a worship song ever grabbed your attention in the way this one did for Caitlin? If so, which one and why?

When you think about God as your heavenly Father, or about you being a "child of God," how does that make you feel? Why? What thoughts or questions come to mind?

I. **Read** Romans 8:13–17.

What does it mean to live "according to the flesh"? How do you think you could "put to death the misdeeds of the body"? Why would the Holy Spirit be vital in this effort?

____

____

____

____

____

What do you think it means to be led by the Spirit of God? What are other ways to be led that contrast with being led by the Spirit?

____

____

____

____

In verse 15, Paul set up a contrast. On one side is slavery to fear; on the other is "adoption to sonship." What do you think these two things mean?

____

____

____

When the Bible was written, the presumed reader was male, but we know these principles apply to both "sons" *and* "daughters" of God. Calling God *Abba*, Father" is like saying "Daddy." It's close and intimate and loving. Do you relate with God as "Father" or as "Daddy"? How comfortable are you with the idea of being a son or a daughter of God? Explain.

Jesus is the ultimate Son of God, and Paul said we are "co-heirs" with Jesus. What is an heir? What does that role entitle someone to on earth? What might we be heirs to in God's kingdom? Why did Paul mention Christ's suffering?

II. Read Galatians 3:26 — 4:7.

According to this passage, how are we made sons and daughters of God? Once we become children of God, how does that impact the categories humans use to describe themselves—Jew or Gentile, male or female, etc.?

____

____

____

____

Again, Paul contrasted slaves and sons. What are the differences in rights and responsibilities between sons and "slaves" or servants?

____

____

____

____

Paul said that sons aren't very different from slaves when they are children. They are under the father's authority. And before Jesus, humanity was trapped in the systems of the world. But Jesus changed everything. How did things change because of Jesus? What did Paul say is the role of the Holy Spirit in that change?

____

____

____

____

____

III. Read 1 John 3:1.

What does the word *lavished* mean? What would "lavish love" look like?

____

____

____

How does this idea of a God of lavish love adopting us as sons and daughters because of Christ's death and resurrection line up with your thoughts and feelings about God? Is that something you have considered or felt before? Or does it seem foreign, unlikely, or impossible? Explain.

____

____

____

____

In what sense does our new status as God's children cause us to be alienated from the world so that others do not "know" us?

____

____

____

____

Great Parents

Some people with abusive or absent fathers can be resistant to the idea of a heavenly Father because of their personal experiences. Others may cling to the idea of a perfect heavenly Father as a contrast to what they have experienced. Folks with controlling or authoritarian parents can view God as an ever-watchful police officer waiting to catch them in sin so they can be punished. But over and over the Bible tells us about the lavish, never-ending love of God.

Describe a perfect earthly parent. What qualities does this person have? How does she or he show love? How does such a parent handle rule-breaking and punishment?

____

____

____

____

____

____

The Bible shows us examples of both good and bad parenting qualities. Some of the bad ones include favoritism (Gen 37:3–4) and a lack of discipline and correction (1 Sam 3:13). What qualities of good parenting do you find in the following biblical examples?

Hannah (1 Sam 1:24–28)

____

____

Eunice (2 Tim 1:5)

____

____

Joseph (Matt 2:13–23)

____

____

The father in the Parable of the Prodigal Son (Luke 15:20)

____

____

How is God the best example of a perfect parent? Give an example from your life of God's parental love for you.

____

____

____

____

____

____

____

Great Gifts

In Matthew 7:7–12, Jesus told his listeners that they could ask God for what they needed in prayer and God would respond. The evidence Jesus gave for this is the relationship of parents to their children. Proper parents would never give their son or daughter a rock when the child was hungry and asking for bread. That would be cruel and heartless. Even in our sinful, fallen nature, most parents know the difference between a good gift and a bad one. But God, who is perfect, is an even more reliable gift-giver. He is our Father in heaven who gives good gifts to those who ask.

What is a great gift you have received from a parent or given to a child? Was it a surprise or was it requested? How does it feel to give a highly desired, perfect gift? How does it feel to receive exactly what you need?

Have you ever asked God for something and received exactly what you asked for? Have you ever received more? How about less or nothing at all? Explain.

____

____

____

____

____

____

When might a good parent *not* give a child what she or he wants?

____

____

____

____

____

Receiving God's Love

During lunch with Pastor Mike and Tonya, Caitlin shared that it had been a while since she had been to church. Her Bible was a gift from her grandmother who had passed away last year. Caitlin had a difficult childhood at home, but with her grandmother she always felt loved, safe, and seen.

"It sounds as if your relationship with your grandmother is the one you should consider when you think of God," Tonya said, "since she always made you feel welcome and loved. That's your heavenly Father. You are his lavishly loved daughter—all the time, no matter what."

Who in your life has loved you like Caitlin's grandmother? What did that look like? How did this person's love make you feel?

On a scale of 1 to 5, how much do you identify with being God's child? A *1* might be "I don't feel like God's child" or "That's too hard to wrap my mind around." A *5* might be "I am secure in the idea that God loves me as his child." If you are a *4* or a *5*, how did you get there? If your number is lower, what are you still wrestling with?

Closing Prayer

Thank you, God, for your lavish love that washes over us. You see us as your beloved children. You care for us. You rejoice over us with singing. You respond to our cries. You delight in us as our good, good Father. Please help us embrace this love and this truth that we are yours. Help us rest in that identity, living each day as beloved children of God. Amen. ◼

I Was Created for a Purpose

Psalm 138; Psalm 139:13–16; Ephesians 2:10

Main Point

God has made every person on earth on purpose and for a purpose; no one is a mistake.

Background

As God's children, we begin to see that we are lavishly loved and cared for. The next step is to know that we exist on purpose. The Psalms show us that God made each of us intentionally. We have good bodies and good minds to put to good use for God's good purposes. It wasn't just people in the Bible whom God wanted to use. God wants to use each of us in our own ways to do his work on earth. The apostle Paul said that we are God's masterpieces and that God has work for us to do—work he has planned for each of us.

Spiritual Parents

As Caitlin and Tonya sat waiting for their coffee and talking, Caitlin shared about her grandmother's relationship with Jesus. He was a matter-of-fact part of her life. When she talked about Jesus, it was as if she was talking about an old friend she might call on the phone.

"Sounds like you miss her a lot," Tonya said.

Caitlin blinked back tears. "The last time I talked to her, I told her how lost and adrift I had been feeling. Now that she's gone, who do I turn to?" She pulled her Bible out of her bag, brushing her fingers across the cover. "We found this in my grandmother's things with my name on it. She wrote inside it, 'Psalm 139—for Caitlin.' I've tried reading it, but I don't know what she was trying to tell me."

Who are the spiritual "mothers" or "fathers" in your life? Who has been an example of a life of faith for you as Caitlin's grandmother was to her?

____

____

____

Has anyone ever given you a Bible verse just for you? Have you ever felt that God put a verse in your path for a specific moment or season? What verse? Describe the situation.

____

____

____

I. **Read** Psalm 138.

What are the qualities of God that come to your mind when you praise him? What about God makes you feel grateful?

____

____

____

____

Think of a time God walked you through a season of "trouble." Describe the situation. How did God save you in that season—physically, emotionally, mentally, and/or spiritually?

____

____

____

____

In the midst of saying that God had a purpose for him, the psalmist affirmed God's love for him. How do love and purpose go together?

____

____

____

____

What would you say God's purpose is for your life? How do you find that purpose? Where do you see God at work through your purpose?

How does it feel to read that God won't "abandon" the work he is doing in your life? Why?

II. Read Psalm 139:13–16.

Your existence on this earth—at this moment in time—is not a mistake. As you read these verses, what do you notice? What surprises you? How do they make you feel? Why?

What does it mean to be "fearfully and wonderfully made"? How does that expression make you feel about yourself? Explain.

____

____

____

____

Our culture can trap us into feeling ashamed of the bodies God gave us. Are there parts of your physical appearance, your body, that you don't like? How does the idea of being "fearfully and wonderfully made" line up with your feelings about your body? Why?

____

____

____

____

List some things that are good about your body such as its strength, its mobility, or its intricate design. Do these things come to mind readily, or is it difficult to think of good things? Where might you need to shift your thinking about your body? What does your body allow you to do for God?

____

____

____

____

Think for a moment about the idea that all the days of your life were planned and seen by God before you took your first breath. What thoughts and feelings does that stir up inside you? Why?

____

____

____

____

III. Read Ephesians 2:10.

What is "handiwork"? Give an example. What classifies something as handiwork?

____

____

____

____

Some Bible translations say here that we are God's "masterpiece." What is a masterpiece? Do you think that describes you? Why or why not? When do you _feel_ like a masterpiece?

____

____

____

____

Where do you enjoy serving at your church or at home or in your community? Why do you choose those acts of service? How do you feel equipped to do them? By training? By personality? By passion?

____

____

____

____

____

How does it feel to read that, long ago, God planned good works for you to do with the life, gifts, and passions he gave you? Why?

____

____

____

____

Prepared to Act

When Isaiah encountered God face-to-face, he was overcome by the weight of his sin. But when the Lord asked who would go and speak to God's people, Isaiah said, "Here am I. Send me!" (Isa 6:8).

When God called Moses to secure the release of the Israelites, Moses wasn't eager. Moses pointed out to God all the reasons God should not choose him (Ex 3—4).

When God called the prophet Jeremiah, Jeremiah said he was too young and didn't know how to do the job. But God knew Jeremiah was exactly the guy for the job—he'd been created for it (Jer 1:5)!

Whether we feel prepared or not, God has plans to be accomplished. And he's chosen humanity—us—to carry out those plans.

What tasks have you done for God? Which ones did you feel prepared for? Which ones did you feel ill-prepared for? Did your preparedness or feelings change the outcome? Explain.

All of the people listed here did what God asked, even if they felt out of their league. God helped them every time, performing miracles and giving them the words to speak. What is God asking you to do for him? How will you respond?

Gifted to Serve

After Jesus ascended to heaven (Acts 1:9), his followers had to deal with a guy named Saul. Saul was a Pharisee. The Pharisees followed extremely strict rules for Jewish behavior, and they expected everyone else to follow their rules, too. Saul believed that in order to honor God he needed to destroy the followers of Jesus.

While Saul was hunting for Christians to arrest, Jesus spoke to him. The Lord said of Saul, "This man is my chosen instrument to proclaim my name to the Gentiles [non-Jews] and their kings and to the people of Israel" (Acts 9:15).

It was radical for God to choose a guy who wanted Christians killed to become one of their biggest leaders. But Saul's life and experiences made him the perfect person to talk to Jews *and* Gentiles about Jesus.

Why was Saul (later known as Paul) such a great choice for God to use for his purposes? What skills, contacts, experiences, and opportunities might he have brought to this calling?

____

____

____

____

____

Have you ever worked or volunteered for something that was perfect for you? Describe the situation. How did God's purpose for you there line up perfectly with your skills, experiences, gifts, and passions?

Made for a Purpose

"Psalm 139? That's a good one!" Tonya exclaimed to Caitlyn. "I love all the examples of how much God loves me. Here, let's take a look." Tonya turned the Bible so she and Caitlin could look together. They talked about the verses that say God made each of us and planned our days. Tonya said, "Sometimes I have struggled to remember how much God cares for me. Psalm 139 is a great reminder that God made me on purpose, and for a purpose."

Caitlin pulled the Bible closer. "Maybe that's why my grandmother marked this for me."

What verses and Bible stories from this lesson impacted you the most? What can you do to make sure you don't forget them? Perhaps you could write out a couple of verses and put them in a place where you'll see them every day. Maybe you could journal about what God is saying to you about your purpose. Perhaps you could follow through on an opportunity God is prompting you to undertake with your gifts, skills, and passions. Choose one of these ways or another way you think of. Why does this idea resonate with you?

Closing Prayer

God, it is stunning to think that you made us for a purpose. You are the God who made the universe! You raised Jesus from the dead. You called spiritual heavyweights such as Moses, Isaiah, Jeremiah, Paul, Esther, Ruth, Elizabeth, and Mary. Who are we that you would also have a plan and purpose for us? Help us live each day as your masterpieces, created to do the good things you have planned for us because you love us. Amen.■

I Am Seen and Known

Psalm 139:1–10; Genesis 16:7–10, 13

Main Point

God knows us better than anyone else, even ourselves, and he pays attention to us like that because he loves us.

Background

We are God's children and his masterpieces. We know we exist for a reason. God knew us even before we were born. He knows the hurts and hopes of our hearts. He keeps an eye on us out of love, and he walks with us through life's successes and messes. He sees past the masks we wear straight through to our hearts. And we can trust him to want what is best for us. The writer of Psalm 139 and Hagar the slave celebrated how well God knew them. Having his eye on them made them feel loved and secure.

God Is Watching!

Caitlin waited in the coffee shop for Tonya, her Bible open and a scowl on her face. "What's up?" Tonya asked, sitting down across the table. "You seem unhappy."

Caitlin took a deep breath. "It's this Psalm 139. I've been reading it since last time, and frankly, I don't like it so much. God searches me and knows me? I thought God wasn't watching and waiting to catch me messing up, but it's right here. God is following me everywhere I go. It creeps me out! Is he lurking around, waiting to pounce on me like one of those helicopter parents who can't let their kids do anything they want? I don't know that I want God in my business like that!"

What do you think about the phenomenon of "helicopter parents"? Are they protective and helpful or intrusive and suffocating? Explain.

Do you know any people who use a tracking app to keep tabs on their kids or their elderly parents? Are these apps useful tools or an invasion of privacy? Why do you say so?

Do you ever feel like Caitlin—that God is looking over your shoulder ready to pounce if you step out of line? Explain.

I. **Read** Psalm 139:1–4.

Have you ever had a friend who knew you so well that she or he could finish your sentences or anticipate your needs? How does it feel to be known and understood to that degree? Explain.

____

____

____

____

How does it feel to think God has "searched you"? What would he find? Would anything he finds surprise him? Why do you say so?

____

____

____

____

When you read these verses, do they feel comforting or invasive? Do you like the idea that God knows your routines and even knows your words before you do? Explain.

____

____

____

II. Read Psalm 139:5–10.

When people have a baby, they usually baby-proof the house before the little tyke becomes mobile. Are they being controlling? Are they violating the baby's independence? Or are they putting up protective barriers and guardrails to keep the child safe? Explain.

____

____

____

____

____

When you read these verses, does it feel as if God is "hemming" you in as a gift or a punishment? Does it seem to you that the psalmist was saying this attention from God is good or bad? Explain.

____

____

____

____

____

When babies have trouble sleeping, one solution is to swaddle them, which means wrapping them in a blanket like a little burrito. It gives a sense of being held close and helps some babies get to sleep. What other examples can you think of where being held, being hemmed in, or being seen and noticed are good things?

____

____

____

III. Read Genesis 16:7–10.

God promised Abram and Sarai that they would someday have a child. Tired
of waiting, Sarai suggested that Abram have a child with her servant, Hagar.
When Hagar became pregnant, it caused conflict between the two women—
it was a mess. Have you ever tried to rush God's promises along? Describe the
situation. How did that work out? What messes developed, if any?

____

____

____

____

Hagar ran away and an angel found her. What do you imagine that experience was like? Did Hagar act as if it were a big deal? How would you feel if
an angel of God found you in the middle of a crisis? Explain.

____

____

____

____

What did the angel promise Hagar if she humbled herself and went back to Sarai? What would you have done in Hagar's situation? Why?

IV. Read Genesis 16:13.

Imagine that God plopped down next to you while you were on the run, and he told you everything that was going on with you and described everything you were thinking and feeling. Would it feel helpful or invasive? Explain.

Hagar named God! A servant, a slave, used by her masters to jumpstart God's plan on their own terms, gave God a new name: El Roi, The God Who Sees Me. What might Hagar have been feeling that would lead her to give God this new name?

Beyond First Impressions

When God called the prophet Samuel to anoint a new king, Samuel knew the new king would be a son of a man named Jesse. When he saw Jesse's first-born, he was sure Eliab would be the next king. Eliab looked the part. But God told Samuel not to be fooled by outward appearances: "I have rejected him. The Lord does not look at the things people look at. People look at the outward appearance, but the Lord looks at the heart" (1 Sam 16:7). So Samuel anointed God's choice, Jesse's youngest son, David, who was later known as "a man after [God's] own heart" (Acts 13:22).

Describe a time when, based on your first impression of someone, you thought that person would be a great friend/date/employee and then later discovered that the person's character didn't match her or his appearance or your first impression.

Do you find it comforting or alarming that God looks at—and sees—the heart rather than outward appearances? Why do you feel that way?

____

____

____

If God would examine your heart today, what would he find? What can you do if there are parts of your character that don't make you proud?

____

____

____

Knowing Yourself

There are lots of different personality assessments available to help people better know and understand themselves and others. When used for self-examination, we can discover both positive and negative aspects. The positive things can point us toward skills to develop or ways to put our best foot forward. The negative things can become traits to work on. When these assessments are used to help us understand others, that understanding can be used as a weapon for manipulating them. But in healthy relationships, it can help us show others that they are loved in ways they can best hear it and receive it.

On a scale of 1 to 10, how well do you know yourself? Those on the low end might see traits in themselves and be surprised by them or make excuses for them. Those on the high end might know why they do certain things or may be working to improve their faults. Why did you rate yourself as you did?

____

____

____

____

If you have ever completed a personality study or assessment such as the Myers-Briggs, the DISC, or the Enneagram, what were the results? How did the new knowledge help you understand yourself in better or useful ways?

____

____

____

____

Knowing and Loving

"Have you ever known someone who just didn't 'get' you?" Tonya asked.

Caitlin snorted. "Oh, yeah." She told about a blind date her sister planned. The guy worked in the same field Caitlin did, but they still had nothing in common. And he didn't understand her humor or her pop-culture references.

"It sounds as if maybe your sister doesn't know you as well as she might have thought. Now, tell me about the person who knows you best."

"That would be my grandmother," Caitlin replied, explaining all the ways her grandmother knew her and understood her—sometimes even better than Caitlin understood herself.

"Think of how your grandmother loved you and understood you," Tonya said, "then read Psalm 139 again."

What's more natural for you, to read the Bible and hear God's voice as criticism and condemnation or to hear love, care, and concern? Why?

Who in your life has truly seen you, known you, understood you, and loved you? How does it feel to spend time with this person? If your instinct is to see and hear condemnation, how does the tone of the Bible text change if you keep this example of love and acceptance in mind?

Closing Prayer

God, you see us and you know us. Like Hagar, you can see us when we find ourselves in the middle of life's messes—lost, alone, and despairing. Like David, you see past a happy face and even carefully constructed social media to see the real person. Like the psalmist, wherever we go you are with us. We will never be alone because we always have you. You are El Roi, the God who truly sees us. Thank you. Amen. ∎

L 4

I Am Forgiven

Romans 7:18 — 8:2; John 8:1–11

Main Point

God wants us to live free from the weight of our sin and from the burden of unforgiveness when others cause us pain.

Background

God gave the Israelites the Law so they would know how to behave in order to have a relationship with a holy God. But he didn't just give them a bunch of rules. He also gave them the sacrificial system that would allow them to be reconciled back to their community and back to God when they had violated his law. Jesus was the fulfillment of this sacrificial system. Because of his death for our sins, our debt to God has been paid in full. We don't need the sacrificial system anymore. Because of Christ, we can live forgiven and free.

Struggling with Forgiveness

Caitlin chatted with Pastor Mike after the worship service. "That app you recommended has been great!" she said. "It gives me a verse or two every morning. It's not too much or overwhelming."

"That's terrific!" Pastor Mike replied. "What verse did it give you today?"

Caitlin pulled up the app on her phone. "It's a tough one, Romans 8:1 and 2—'Therefore, there is now no condemnation for those who are in Christ Jesus, because through Christ Jesus the law of the Spirit who gives life has set you free from the law of sin and death.'"

Pastor Mike asked, "What do you think about that?"

Caitlin sighed. "It's tough! I get the sin and death part. I know I'm a sinner, and I regret many things I've done. It's hard to believe God could love me considering my past."

Pastor Mike nodded. "Those verses are talking about an important part of life with God—forgiveness. Let's discuss this a little more."

What words come to mind when you think of the word *sin*? What about when you think of *forgiveness*? Why?

Are some sins worse than others? Are there any that are unforgiveable? Does forgiveness ever seem impossible? Explain.

I. **Read** Romans 7:18 — 8:2.

What difference did Paul outline between what he wanted to do and what he actually did?

Paul was a major figure in the New Testament church, and still he struggled. What is the thing he said can save us from this struggle?

Romans 8:1 starts with "Therefore," so we have to connect that verse with what came before. How would you summarize Romans 7:18–25?

What reason did Paul give for why there is no condemnation for followers of Jesus? What does this mean for us?

When the teachers of the Law and Pharisees asked Jesus questions, they rarely had his best interests at heart. What do you think this interaction was really about—the woman's sin? Jesus? both? or something else altogether? Explain.

____

____

____

____

What was the purpose of the Law of Moses for the Jewish people? How was the Law being used here?

____

____

____

____

Verse 2 says all the people had gathered around to hear Jesus. If you had been in the crowd, what might you have been thinking when the leaders walked in and started this conversation with Jesus?

____

____

____

Who was missing in this scene? Why do you think this person was missing? If the Pharisees were serious about righting a wrong according to the Law, how would the absence of this other individual have impacted their case?

What benefit is gained in publicly calling out someone's sin? Is it ever right to do so? What harm is done? Who leaves such a confrontation feeling superior? Who feels shame? Explain.

III. Read John 8:6–8.

What trap were the teachers of the Law and the Pharisees trying to set for Jesus? What was their goal? What role did the woman play in their trap?

Why do you think Jesus wrote on the ground instead of responding right away? What do you think he was writing? How might the Pharisees have interpreted his silence?

What impact do you think Jesus' response would have had on his authority with the crowd? Why?

Why do you think the older accusers walked away first? Think about the first man to leave the crowd and walk away—what might he have been thinking?

____

____

____

____

Do you think those who walked away did so because they felt shame or guilt about their own sin, because Jesus thwarted their plans, or for some other reason? Explain.

____

____

____

____

This woman had been used by the Pharisees in their fight with Jesus. She had been publicly shamed, alone. And she was caught in sin, breaking one of the Ten Commandments. What tone do you imagine Jesus used with her in verses 10 and 11? Why would he speak to her in that way?

____

____

____

____

Forgive and Forget?

Sometimes it's difficult to "forgive and forget." Few people are fully trusting of those who have hurt or betrayed them before. They remember, and that experience determines how they proceed in the future. Abuse survivors are often plagued by flashbacks and emotional struggles that make it impossible to forget what they have endured.

The Bible is clear that we are to forgive others. Jesus told his disciples they should forgive repeatedly if someone sins against them and repents (Luke 17:4). It's not for the other person's sake, but for our own. Jesus never said we have to forget, though.

God is perhaps the only one who can truly forgive *and* forget. He is the one who "blots out" our transgressions and "remembers [our] sins no more" (Isa 43:25).

Think about a time you were hurt by someone and were able to forgive this person. Describe the experience. How did it feel to forgive and let go of the hurt or anger?

What factors can make forgiveness difficult? Why?

How is your life impacted when you harbor unforgiveness? How is your offender harmed when you hold a grudge?

Faithful to Forgive

Luke 15 contains the Parable of the Prodigal Son. The son squandered all of his inheritance and encountered a famine. In desperation he decided to head home—not to get his place as "son" back but hoping just to be a servant in his father's house. He even prepared a speech, confessing his sin and acknowledging how far he had fallen.

First John 1:9 tells us that when we confess our sins, God is "faithful and just" and he will forgive us. We are like the prodigal son, coming home with heads bowed in shame. The father in the story is God. The father runs out to meet his son, not with condemnation but with love. He restores his son back into the family and celebrates his return. That is how God feels about *you* when you confess your sin and ask for forgiveness. He showers you with love, welcomes you with open arms, and forgives you.

Confession, even just between you and God, can be scary. We would often rather hide what we've done instead of dragging it into the light of day. How does it feel to have your sin out in the open with God? Why?

Breaking the Cycle

Pastor Mike pointed to Romans 8:1. "Paul was kind of an expert on living a life that honors Jesus. And he was so honest! Right before Romans 8, he talked about how often he messed up. He was like, 'I don't do the things I want to do, but I keep doing the stuff I don't want to do.'"

Caitlin laughed. "*That* I get!"

"Right?" Mike responded. "But Paul said we can be rescued from that crazy cycle. Because of Jesus, we can be free from the hold of sin. We aren't condemned by our bad choices anymore. And that freedom feels great!"

Caitlin nodded. "I'm starting to see that while God does have rules for me; he's also ready to help me get back on track if I break them."

When you've sinned, how do you picture God's response? How do you imagine God responds when we confess? Why?

Since Jesus will forgive us, does that mean our sin doesn't matter? Can we do whatever we want? Explain.

____

____

____

If there are sins in your past that you haven't confessed or relationships in your life that are fractured, how can you pursue forgiveness and reconciliation in those situations?

____

____

____

____

Closing Prayer

God, we are so grateful that we are yours. You've said we are your children and that you created us for a purpose. You see us and you know us—all the good and all the bad. And you forgive us. We love how free we feel when we can leave our sin and our hurt with you so we don't have the burden of it anymore. Thank you for the gift of your forgiveness. Amen. ■

L 5

I Am Gifted

1 Corinthians 12:1–11, 14–20, 27–30

Main Point

God, through the Holy Spirit, has given every believer gifts as he chooses to use for the building up of the church.

Background

Paul felt it was important to tell the church at Corinth about spiritual gifts. He knew that their lives before they heard about Jesus would influence how they understood a life of faith. He wanted them to be knowledgeable and informed. They needed to know how the Spirit works, and that it's *one* Spirit, the same Spirit, who gives the gifts as the Spirit chooses. While people's gifts might be different, they are all from the same source and for one purpose. Paul wanted them (and us) to understand that the gifts are for building up the body of Christ, not for the egos of the gifted.

Ready to Serve

"I'm ready to do more," Caitlin said.

"I'm not sure what you mean," Tonya said.

"Well, I've been coming here for a few months. I feel like I'm starting to understand my Bible and more about God. I know the church is doing tons of things here and in the community. And I'm ready to pitch in somewhere."

"That's great, Caitlin! There's certainly plenty to do." Tonya smiled. "What have you been thinking about doing? What are your gifts and passions?"

"I have no idea. Everything sounds important and every event or ministry is looking for volunteers. I don't know where to start. And I don't think I really have any"—Caitlyn made quote marks with her fingers—"gifts."

"God gives every believer gifts to do his work," Tonya said. "Let's see if we can help you find out what yours might be."

What are three gifts or skills you have for serving others? Where do those gifts come from?

Where are you serving in your congregation or community? What do you enjoy about your service? How does your service make use of your gifts and passions?

I. Read 1 Corinthians 12:1–6.

Why is it important to understand that the various gifts come from the same source? Why would God not want to give every person all of the gifts?

____

____

____

____

What would have been the significance of the pagan roots of the believers in Corinth? How might those roots have impacted their understanding of spiritual gifts?

____

____

____

____

II. Read 1 Corinthians 12:7–10.

Who gets gifts or "manifestations" of the Spirit from God? Why might some people feel as if they were skipped when God handed out gifts?

____

____

____

What purpose did Paul give for why we have gifts? Give an example of a gift and its use.

____

____

____

____

Have you ever been part of a ministry or a service opportunity and seen someone working well in an area where she or he was gifted? How did it help the project? Describe the situation.

____

____

____

____

____

Have you ever tried to serve in a way that was *not* a match for your gifts? If so, describe the situation. How did that feel? How is it different from doing something you are gifted to do?

____

____

____

____

Repetition is used by writers in the Bible to make a point. What point was Paul making in verses 8 and 9 about what the gifts have in common?

____

____

____

____

III. Read 1 Corinthians 12:11.

Paul's letters in the Bible aren't stand-alone documents. They are part of a larger conversation Paul had both in person with the church and through the letters that were written to him. Why do you think Paul emphasized that the gifts come from one Spirit? What might his readers have believed that he needed to respond to?

____

____

____

____

It would be false to say that only the financially gifted need to give to the church or that those who are gifted in hospitality are the only ones who can be welcoming. What do you think the difference is between a spiritual gift and a responsibility of everyone in the church?

____

____

____

____

____

IV. Read 1 Corinthians 12:14–20, 27–30.

What point was Paul making with this body metaphor? Whom did Paul say
has arranged the parts? Why is that an important fact? Have you ever seen
jealousy among the different parts of the church body? If so, describe the
situation.

____

____

____

What do you notice about the list of gifts in verse 28 as compared to the list
in verses 8 through 10? What do the lists have in common? Where are they
different? Should we expect to see each one of these gifts represented in a
particular local church? If so, why? If not, why not?

____

____

____

What point do you think Paul was trying to make in verses 29–30?

____

____

If you've ever wondered if you have any spiritual gifts, God's Word is clear that you do. Every believer is equipped to help the body of Christ. If you aren't sure what your gifts are, there are several inventories available that can help you determine what they are. Some even distinguish between "working" gifts—gifts you are already using—and "waiting gifts"—those you might be inclined to but haven't tested yet.

Make a list of the gifts mentioned in the following four passages:

1 Corinthians 12:7–11

____

____

1 Corinthians 12:28

____

____

Romans 12:6–8

____

____

Ephesians 4:11–13

____

____

Why do you think the four lists are different? Who wrote the lists in 1 Corinthians and the lists in Romans and Ephesians? What could we infer about the list of available gifts if the same list isn't given every time?

____

____

____

____

Have you ever completed a spiritual gifts inventory? If so, what was your experience with the process? What did it tell you? What action, if any, did you take with the results?

____

____

____

____

Prior to Paul listing the gifts in Romans 12, he said in verse 3, "Do not think of yourself more highly than you ought." What was Paul warning against?

____

____

____

____

____

The Purpose of Gifts

Paul wasn't the only one who wrote about spiritual gifts. The apostle Peter, who was one of Jesus' disciples, mentioned them, too.

In one of his letters, Peter encouraged his readers to use whatever gifts they had to serve one another. But we don't serve out of our own strength or ego—we do so from God's power: "If anyone speaks, they should do so as one who speaks the very words of God. If anyone serves, they should do so with the strength God provides, so that in all things God may be praised through Jesus Christ" (1 Peter 4:11).

Looking at 1 Peter 4:10–11, what is the purpose of a spiritual gift? Who should receive the glory for the work accomplished through these gifts?

Peter didn't give a list as Paul did. What was Peter's emphasis instead? How does his advice apply to all the gifts?

Give an example of a gift you have. How might Peter have described it here?

Pick a ministry or two in your church—something such as working with youth or ushering or helping with a food ministry. What are some gifts that would be useful in that ministry? Try to think of ones that might be less obvious.

How does it feel to know that the Holy Spirit has chosen gifts specifically for you and for this moment in your life? Explain.

Closing Prayer

Father, we are in awe of all you are showing us. We are your children, created for a purpose. You see us and know us. You forgive us when we confess our sins, and you have gifted us so we can serve your people. We are amazed that you would partner with us to help others and share your love. Thank you for showing us who we are and how you have chosen to work in and through us. Amen. ∎

I Am Loved

Luke 23:26–56; 1 John 4:7–19; Ephesians 2:4–9; 3:16–19

Main Point

Our identity in Christ and all the things God does for us flow out of God's love for us.

Background

The apostle John wanted his readers to grasp the love of God because everything else—everything in the Bible as well as in our everyday lives—is built on that foundation. For John, the evidence of God's love was clear and simple. We see it in the life, death, and resurrection of Jesus. If we ever have cause to question if God loves us, we only have to think of Jesus and we have our answer. The apostle Paul prayed for his readers to be able to grasp the fullness of the love of Jesus. Paul knew it would be hard to understand, but so vital to our lives.

Secure in Christ

Who are *you* in Jesus? What do you believe about God's love for you? Are there parts you aren't sure you believe yet, places you are still working on? Explain.

____

____

____

Do you *really* know that God loves you? Is it nothing more than a fact to you because you've read it or heard it? Or is it true in the very core of your being? Do you live every day from that place of security, knowing you are loved? Explain.

____

____

I. **Read** Luke 23:26–56.

When we think of the crucifixion story, we often use feeling words such as *angry* or *sad* or *grief*. What examples of *love* do you see in this passage—the love displayed by people but also the love displayed by God and Jesus Christ?

____

____

____

____

II. **Read** 1 John 4:7–19.

Love is the key word, the theme of this passage. What did John say is the source of love? How is that shown in our relationships with others? From this passage, why would it be important for Christians to be loving toward others?

____

____

____

____

According to John, what is the evidence that God loves us? How is that evidence more powerful than just words?

____

____

____

What did John say was the purpose of Jesus' life? Why was Jesus sent to earth? How did that show God's love for us?

____

____

____

____

____

Why is the important thing here not our love of God but rather God's love for us? What should our response be to this act of love by God? What is the result of us loving one another? How does this allow us to "see" God?

____

____

____

____

____

According to John, what happens when we acknowledge Jesus as the Son of God?

____

____

In verse 16, what is the connection between God and those who "live in love"? What do you think living in love looks like?

____

____

____

____

____

John said that "perfect love drives out fear" (v 18). What do you fear about life with Christ? How does God's love respond to your fear?

____

____

____

____

____

Why is it important that God is our model of love?

____

____

____

____

III. Read Ephesians 2:4–9.

How would you summarize this passage?

____

____

____

____

What qualities of God are described in this passage? Why does God make us "alive with Christ" (v 5) in spite of our sin?

____

____

____

____

Why would God, through Christ, save us? How are we saved? Who does the saving and why?

____

____

____

____

____

Why are we not saved by our own effort? If our works don't save us, do we still need to do them? Why or why not?

____

____

____

____

IV. Read Ephesians 3:16–19.

What do you think Paul meant by "being rooted and established in love" (v 17)?

____

____

____

____

Paul's letters often spell out ways he prayed for God's people. What did Paul pray for the Ephesians?

____

____

____

____

Why would Paul need to pray that the Ephesians would grasp the extent of God's love? If he had to pray for it, does such understanding come naturally or easily? Explain.

In what ways does this passage impact how you think about God's love?

Coming Back to God

Romans 5:8 says, "God demonstrates his own love for us in this: While we were still sinners, Christ died for us." While we were still slaves to sin, lost in our own desires, God made a way for us back to himself. It's like we were pouting, defiant children in the corner and God reached out a hand to draw us back to him. But he won't force us. He doesn't pick us up out of the chair. He only holds out a hand and says, "Come." We have to take his hand and accept what he offers. The love is already there, waiting for us to accept it.

Romans 10:9 says, "If you declare with your mouth, 'Jesus is Lord,' and believe in your heart that God raised him from the dead, you will be saved." Do you believe Jesus carried the weight of *your* sin to the cross and bore your punishment so you could be reconciled to God? Have you ever made such a confession of faith or prayed and asked Jesus to save you from your sin? If so, describe the experience and the difference it has made. If not, what is holding you back?

God's Unconditional Love

Sometimes we forget about God's forgiveness and the fact that he removes our sins from us "as far as the east is from the west" (Ps 103:12). We think our sin means God can't love us. But in addition to all the Bible passages on forgiveness, Paul's words in Romans 8 tell us that *nothing* can separate us from God's love: "For I am convinced that neither death nor life, neither angels nor demons, neither the present nor the future, nor any powers, neither height nor depth, nor anything else in all creation, will be able to separate us from the love of God that is in Christ Jesus our Lord" (vv 38–39).

Is there anything you have ever thought would separate you from God's love that doesn't pass Paul's test? Are there any gaps in his list? Explain.

How might people live differently when they live from the knowledge that God loves them no matter what?

Embracing Your Identity

"Pastor Mike asked me to share my testimony." Caitlin took a shaky breath. "When I lost my grandmother, I thought I lost the only voice of love in my life. She was the one who knew me best and understood me. She would call me out if I wasn't making good choices, but her correction always came from a place of love. Without her, I thought I wouldn't feel loved again. But then I started learning about God. Did you know God thinks of you as his son or daughter, that he made you on purpose and for a purpose? I know those things now. God sees me and knows me and forgives me. The Holy Spirit has given me gifts so I can serve others. And God sent Jesus to die for my sins so I could be free. That's how much God loves me. And he loves you, too."

Which of the six identity statements from this study has been the easiest for you to believe? Why?

Which statement has been the most difficult to believe? What roadblocks are you encountering? What action steps can you take to more fully embrace your identity in Christ?

Closing Prayer

God, we want to bask in your love for us. You know us so well—the good and the bad—and you still love us. Nothing can separate us from your love. Please help us grow in our understanding of how wide and long and high and deep your love is. Thank you, Jesus, for loving us so much that you went to the cross. Help us live in ways that honor your sacrifice for us. Amen. ◼

Notes